Ham Shanks and Mushy Peas.

ISBN 978-0-9955799-7-2

Published by R J Weaver 2023

The right of R J Weaver to be identified as the author and illustrator of this work has been asserted by him in accordance with the Copyright Designs and Patents Act 1986.

A CIP catalogue record for this book is available from the British Library

'A Dog is for Life, not just for?'

On a cold windy day; a long, long time ago, my stepfather turned up late one evening with a black and white puppy that he said was not going to be of any use as a sheep-dog and that the owner of the farm he had worked at that day wanted to get rid of it.

We only ever had two dogs during our growing up years. Cindy, a long-haired Welsh corgi was our second dog. This one though was the first dog we ever had in our house. What a fuss that puppy had from Mum and us, her children, when it came into our lives for the first time. We all loved it from the very beginning but my step-dad didn't, not after that first night and we couldn't understand why. We were a bit taken aback after about half an hour of fussing over the new arrival when my step-father shouted angrily. "That'll Do!" We went upstairs out of his way.

The following morning as soon as he had gone; we all went downstairs to find the puppy in a corner of the kitchen. There was another fuss made and a lot of discussion about what we should call it. Some of us wanted to call it 'Spot' or 'Ben' and then a friendly discussion broke out as to what we should call it, like Bengie, Collie, Tex, Billy, Rover, Blackie, Bob, Sam, Rick, Yapyap, Yapyap? "Well…" said my big sister. "It is doing a lot of yapping." And my even older sister, said we should call it Collie because it was a Border Collie after all. Mum settled things by naming him 'Laddie' and then she told us to get our breakfasts and get ready for school.

Semi organised chaos, that's how best to describe breakfast in our house. My sister June nearly always would go to the pantry and get down a jar of jam and then another of us would get the bread and another would get the packet of 'red seal' margarine and our big sister Pauleen would slice the bread. This time the jam was blackberry jam and I have a lifelong association between the pleasures of countryside blackberry picking in the late summer of that year of 1954 with Laddie, our newest family member. I also, strangely enough, have a link to malt extract and cod liver oil, because later that same year was the first winter that I can recall where we had our daily dose of malt extract and cod liver oil. Mum got this from the Clinic along with the tins of 'Cow and Gate' powdered milk for my baby sister Janet. Just before going off to school, Mum would tell us to line up while she opened the big brown jar of malt extract and cod liver oil then she would stick a spoon in; twirl it round and pull out the sticky stuff, one by one we would open our mouths and then, off to school, and yes, it was the same spoon Mum used for each of us. Anyway, back to our dog. The days went by and we got to know Laddie and Laddie got to know all of us, we took it turns to take him for walks, but he was a timid pup and always seemed to be afraid of anything and everything and if something frightened him; he would make a mess, we sometimes had to be quick and get him do his business in the gutter rather than on the footpath. It didn't help when mum and dad argued because Laddie would do a poo or wee in the house if they did. One day, a few weeks later, the week that we had broken up for Christmas, there was a rag and bone man making his way around the council estate shouting out "Rag bone! Any old rag bones! Rag bone..." Dad was angry with Mum again. This was just before he was ready to go to the pub. My big sister did try and get laddie outside in time but she wasn't quick enough. The next minute, dad picked up Laddie and marched out of the house with us following and pleading with him not to hurt our dog... just then the rag and bone man came around the corner shouting, "Any old rag bone!"

Dad went and gave Laddie to the man! And then marched away down the road... Mum and all of us pleaded with the man to have our dog back but the man wouldn't let us... He put our dog up on the cart and tied it there with a bit of string and said something that I have never been able to forget. "What's given is given and can't be given back." Mum and the girls were crying and even me and my brother were crying as we went back home... There is a reasonably happy ending to this story though.

Later that night we were huddled together on the landing at the top of our stairs, Pauleen, June, Annette, Stuart, Janet and me. We had all heard the whimpering at the front door and had gone as far as we dared to go when mum opened the door and in came Laddie all wet and bedraggled looking. He must have sensed where we children were because he came bounding up the stairs to us. I think we all expected dad to get angry again and take Laddie away from us once more, but he didn't, he just stood there with our mum at the bottom of the stairs while we made a fuss of the dog, that had come home, home for Christmas and he stayed with us for many more Christmases after that.

'The Silk Scarf.'

The Women's Voluntary Services, or the WVS, was a very important organisation, before, during, and long after the end of the Second World War. There was a branch in Moody Street Congleton, about halfway up on the left-hand side, past where the library used to be. One day in 1959, a week or so before I was to go up to the big school, Senior Boys school, Mum took me to the WVS because she hadn't much money to spare and I needed a school uniform, of sorts, and I got one, of sorts. There were some shirts. Two white and three blue ones as I recall. And then there were the 'grey flannel' trousers, long ones. "Won't you look smart in grey flannel trousers our Robert?" my Mum kept saying, but I was still pondering on the flannel bit. Back home, we used flannels to wash our face and neck with.

Next came a dark blue gabardine raincoat. My hands wouldn't come out beyond the sleeves when Mum tried it on me and it was a bit long as well, but Mum said that I would "Grow into it, and it will keep me warm and dry in the winter to come." And then there was a genuine Senior Boys Secondary Modern school tie, which was a bit frayed at one end, but this didn't matter; because Mum said that I would be tucking that bit into my trousers anyway. All of this stuff was in a steadily growing pile on the chair beside me. Everything smelled musty in that room and all of the clothes were in wooden 'tea-chests' around the walls and also spread out in a large pile on a big table in the middle of the room. Mum was 'sorting me out' I had only to be there while she went back and forth and came to hold articles of clothing up against me to see if they would fit. Mum seemed happy enough to be doing such as this, so I wasn't bothered, I didn't really know any different. In my eleven years in this world, practically all of my clothes had been second hand. A lot of my younger brother's clothes were 'third hand' having been passed down to him when I had grown out of them, but that was the way of life in those days. We didn't worry about it; we were just glad to have what we had to keep us warm and dry.

Just before we left the building that day, I saw something else on the big table and one of the WVS ladies must have noticed me looking at it. I remember her saying that it was a Paisley silk scarf and that I would look a proper gentleman in it… then she gave it to me… To me!
Mum was pleased that I had got most of what I needed for school wear but I was really delighted with this extra item. Dark red it was and it had what the lady called, "brushed silk tassels at both ends." I really liked that scarf but it didn't stay in my possession for very long.

Mum had washed and ironed my clothes in readiness for going up to the big school and I wanted to wear my scarf to school as well, but Mum said that I should save the scarf for Sunday best, as it might go missing at school.

I never got a chance to wear that red Paisley scarf though, because that Sunday, when we were getting ready for church, I couldn't find the scarf and I remember getting upset over it and then… it slipped out, when my Mum said: - "Oh! Your father has had it and sold it for his beer money!"

Ham Shanks and Mushy Peas

Two phrases stick in my mind that I remember first hearing when I was around five or six years old. The first of the two phrases "It fell off the back of a lorry" always seemed to have had a direct link to food. The other phrase, "Ask no questions and you'll be told no lies!" was often used to put a stop to any inquisitiveness, natural or otherwise,

I never dared ask my stepfather about anything, but I could ask his brother, my Uncle Jim almost anything. One day I asked my Uncle Jim why Lobby was called Lobby and he said: -

"You've heard of Irish Stew? and you've heard of Lancashire Hotpot? Well…! When your mother makes a Lobby, she gets all the ingredients; meat, potatoes, carrots, onions, salt and pepper and such aaand… 'Lobs' it all in a big pan and cooks it… And that's how you get Lobby my lad."

Going back to the first phrase! 'It fell off the back of a lorry.' My stepfather worked for a man called Horace Pointon, the timber man at Congleton and the lorry that my stepdad drove must not have been a very safe one; if the stuff he used to bring home was anything to go by.
As a young lad of five or six I would keep well away from the backs of all the lorries and especially the beer lorries, in case some of those wooden barrels fell off on me. It didn't take me long to get wiser as to the reasoning behind the phrase... 'it fell off the back of a lorry'

My stepdad was rarely a very good father figure, but he was all we had in that respect. He was a reasonably good provider though, especially if it didn't cost him much in the way of money and when he brought stuff home which had 'fallen off the back of a lorry' he was I suppose falling back on natural and primitive instincts, and so were we, his wife, his three children and his three stepchildren, when we would gather around him to see what he had brought home. This went on periodically throughout our growing up years, with no set pattern and we never knew when it would happen. Those times though, were always the best of times, brief as they were; when we were the closest as a family. His mood could quickly change though and after a few minutes of being made a fuss of he would turn and sternly say. "That's enough! Get from under me feet and let your mother get on and do something with it."

This particular 'it' was a large ham shank, and my mother said something like "Ooh! And it's nicely cured… Come on you lot, get out there and play while I get busy."

Thinking back, it's rather strange how excited we children could be over something like a ham shank, I often wonder what it would take to make modern children as happy and excited as we were then; over something as simple as the imminent pleasure of good wholesome food. They have no idea what they are missing.

We never went far from home to play when Mum got busy with a ham shank, or any home cooking. We would try not to get in her way of course, but the tantalising smells that came from the kitchen were like a magnet, always drawing us in. On this occasion Mum let one or two of us watch as she got busy with the large saucepan which covered two of the gas rings on the cooker, and we could see a bit of the bone sticking out at the top as the ham shank bubbled away on the cooker. After a while Mum peeled and cut up potatoes and onions and put them into the big pan with the ham shank, then she put in two whole packets of 'Baxters' Marrowfat Peas.

Eventually, after an hour or so, the feast would be almost ready. Now, Ham Shank and Mushy Peas was always best when it had settled for a bit, so we were told; but none of us could ever wait that long and after what would turn out to be a filling and delicious late evening meal; we would all go to bed happy, and more able to cope with the cold of the long dark winter nights, but then, if we felt thirsty in the night because of the salted ham... Well, we could always break a bit of ice off the inside of our bedroom window.

Racing Pigeons.

Times were hard when I were a lad, not just hardship hard as in being poor; there was the other type... hand and fist hard... Many's the time my stepfather would come home from the pub and think nothing of it to give me a clout, just for getting in his way. Sharing a three-bedroom council house with five siblings and two adults; it was often difficult not to get in his way. In those early years I would try and appease him, if only to try and soften the regular blows. One of the many things I did would be to run up to the shop in Parnell Square to fetch him a packet of fags, Park Drive they were called.

Training his young pigeons was something to look forward to. At least it got me out of the house each night for a few weeks in the springtime.

I would have a pigeon basket with twenty or more young birds in it strapped to the carrier on my old bike and cycle about a mile past Congleton Station and let them out of the basket to find their way home. Then, each evening over the following few weeks, the range would gradually be extended to Whitemoor and then to Biddulph, Knypersley, Brown-Lees, Chatterley Whitfield Colliery and then a bit further to the top of Chell Bank and then all the way to Tunstall Park. There were at least two 'let outs' at each of the places mentioned, but the most arduous one was Tunstall Park, which was about seven miles or so from home.

I would then take the birds to Congleton Station a few times and the young birds would be taken on a train to Stoke, and then to Stafford, to be let out and find their way back. Only after all that training would they be considered ready for the racing season. But only the strongest and fastest flyers would he keep for racing, all the way down to the South coast and even over to Nantes in France. All the others would make pigeon pies for Mr Jones.

If one of my stepdad's pigeons came back late from a race, or didn't match up to his expectations, he wouldn't hesitate in ringing its neck. He would then wrap it up in a bit of newspaper and I would run with the still warm body of the bird in my hands, down to Mr Jones' house in Greenwood Avenue and run hard and fast back home to give the money to my stepdad.

There was one exception to that bit of a grisly tale though… Queenie! Queenie was a pure white pigeon from a really good racing-pigeon bloodline, that we were told, by my stepdad, went all the way back to a particular branch of the bloodline of one of our Queen's birds. Hence the name of Queenie.

My stepfather was very proud of having this particular pigeon in his Loft because our Queen kept racing pigeons as well. And we were all Royalists in our house, every time we would stand to attention whenever we heard the National Anthem on the radio, and even when our Queen came on the radio at Christmas, but then we sat down while she talked to us. And we stood to attention on Armistice Day as well, when the two minutes silence came on the radio, we didn't sit down then though, we all stood up for the whole of the two minutes silence. Anyway, back to Queenie, my step- dad's all-time favourite pigeon. I think it was the summer of 1960 when he decided to send Queenie on the Nantes race. Nantes in France was the furthest distance that Cheshire pigeon men could send any pigeon in those days on a race. He thought she was ready so he sent her.

I remember going with him to help him carry the basket with Queenie and a few others in it, from Dale Crescent, all the way down to the Trade and Labour Club at the bottom of Canal Street and the corner of Chapel Street. One of my sisters, Annette, and my brother Stuart, came with us as well and we sat on a wall in the yard at the back of the Labour Club, sipping a bottle of Vimto between us and watched while all the men went about booking their birds in for the race. There was always paper work to be done first of all before the checking and setting of the pigeon clocks. and then each bird would be taken out of its basket and a rubber ring was put onto one of its legs and then it would be put into another basket and then that basket and other baskets would be put into a big van that they called the Black Maria. And then, off it went and we went home.

The pigeon clock I have just mentioned was the cause of many a row in our house and our mum didn't like it one bit because she always said it was too expensive and the money would be better spent on other things. We were never allowed to even touch it, but this was an essential piece of equipment for a pigeon racing enthusiast in those days. It was a weird contraption, the outer case was mostly made of wood, it had a handle on one side and a locked flap at the back and a couple of holes in the top and one of them with a piece of glass in it with a clock dial behind that. The principle behind the function of the pigeon clock was when a pigeon was seen to come home from a race, the owner would almost frantically call it down and rattle a bit of corn in a tin can and do all sorts, because every single second counted in getting the bird down from the sky in order to get that rubber ring off its leg and put it inside what was called a thimble and put that quickly inside the clock and wind the handle. This would then register the precise moment in time and determine who had won the race.

Two days after the Nantes race was over, one of my sisters came running inside and screamed out that Queenie had come home. We all looked at dad and I remember thinking that he would now go out there and kill her, but he didn't, he kept her instead and used her for breeding the next generation of pigeons, in the hope of winning that all elusive Nantes Cup.

School Dinners.

It was the last week of the summer holidays in 1959. We were standing in front of Mum and Dad. All six of us, Pauleen, June, Annette, Stuart, Janet and me and we were about to get another lecture. Mum first: -

"Now when you all go to school next week you will be getting free school dinners but I don't want you to tell anyone that you are... You are NOT! to tell anyone; do you hear?"

There was no questioning; the likes of 'Why not Mum?' We all knew better than that and besides, my stepdad hadn't said his bit yet. 'Here it comes.'

"And you must not tell your Aunty Madge, your Aunty Dot, Uncle Jim or anyone else... Or by God, I'll put the fear of God in the lot of you and don't any of you think I won't."

There should, perhaps, have been a chorus of six young voices saying. "Yes Mum... Yes Dad." But there wasn't. I don't know what my brother and sisters were thinking but I was thinking about the fear of God. What is the fear of God? Why should we be feared of God? In the Jewish faith God is hellfire and brimstone... Jesus was Jewish... maybe that is what was meant by the fear of God... I didn't know... we are Church of England... Are we supposed to really be afraid of God? Anyway... that lecture didn't work at all... and it was the cause of even more worry, because, at school, we had to line up on that first Monday morning and give our dinner money over to the teacher and I didn't have any dinner money... so, straightaway; everyone knew I would be getting free dinners and I didn't then know just who I should fear the most... God himself or, the fear of God from my Stepdad.

The School Canteen

The hard times continued when I went up to the big school, Senior Boys Secondary Modern. Most of the teachers there turned a blind eye to the bullying. They thought that it was character building and I suppose it was, to a degree... you were either a bully, or you got bullied and battered. There didn't seem to be much else to life in those days.

One day I was hiding amongst the pig-swill bins behind the school canteen, I had managed to keep this hiding place a secret during playtime for a week or two, then one of the canteen ladies came out and saw me. She took me inside. Mrs Findlow was her name, and as dinner time was over she gave me some leftover pudding. The other dinner ladies were nice to me as well that day and the days after as well. It wasn't long before I wanted to find a way to repay their kindness, so I offered to clean the tables between dinner-time sittings and they let me. This was great! I got extra food and on top of that I didn't have to hide in amongst the bins anymore... Then I decided, I was, sort of, by helping Mrs Findlow and the other dinner ladies, that I was helping to pay back whoever it was, that was paying for mine and my brother and sister's school dinners as well. I was more than happy to clean those tables in between sittings. Twice a day for the best part of two years I did that job. None of the other boys volunteered for cleaning the tables. In fact, some of them made even more of a mess for me to clean up, but I didn't care. They didn't get the extra food that I got. And, in that first year at Senior Boys... They didn't get a special extra Christmas pudding; with a shiny sixpence in it, like I did.

Potato Picking.

Looking back, I think that my generation must have been the last one to have witnessed the fading away of an ancient way of life, that of potato picking. Mechanisation came into the harvesting of potatoes somewhere about the late 1950's in this area of Cheshire and only then if the farmer could afford it. Up until then it was an ancient annual custom during the week of autumn half-term, for us children to go to the local farms and help with potato picking. Teachers would read out to the class the names of the farms that wanted us lads to go and work for them. A lot of farmers needed as many of us as they could get to bring the harvest home and most of them paid good money, if you were willing to work hard that is. I remember I got ten shillings for three days of potato picking in that autumn half term of my first year at Senior Boys School.

My two big sisters, Pauleen and June used to go potato picking as well, and they were also at the ending of an ancient tradition. Some of the older farmers allowed the girls to carry home as many potatoes as they could carry in their aprons each day and this was as well as payment in money. But after a hard days' work, most of the girls could only carry a few potatoes home. Us lads were only allowed to take what we could carry in our caps and if you didn't have a cap, then you found one before you went potato picking. I used to borrow my Uncle Jim's cap to go potato picking and to carry my potatoes home in, this was because my stepdad used to moan about his brother and he was always saying that "Jim's got a big head."

My Gran.

Sustainability is not necessarily a modern word, although there are some who seem to think that it is. My Gran's version of sustainability can be summed up in another word, 'Sustenance' and that meant getting enough food inside us to keep us going and sustainability of the food chain was of paramount importance, so much so that 'nothing' absolutely 'nothing,' was wasted in those far off days and the days of my youth and I hope that I can now pass on some of that way of life that was so hard and yet so very good.

The story I would now like to tell you began when I was seven years old. By this time, I was well versed with the frugalities and the importance of having sufficient wholesome food.

I was just about to come out of hospital and going to spend a few days with my Gran. Apparently, according to my mum; this was the fifth time that I had been in and out of the War Memorial Hospital with something called pneumonia in my seven years in this world, and just before leaving that day Sister Knight stood over me and told me, that if I went back into hospital again then they were going to keep me there.

I didn't know it at the time, I don't think that many people did. Certainly not my parents, but looking back on life as it was, it was quite amazing that I survived those bouts of illness at all, when you think that my mother and my stepdad were both heavy smokers, it was probably just as well that I was going to stay for a few days with my Gran. But, like I say, we didn't know about the dangers of smoking in those days, not like they do now.

The Story.

My Gran came to the War Memorial Hospital that warm summer day way back in 1955, and while she was sorting out with the doctors and nurses I was allowed to go and play on the rocking horse. I was getting just a bit too big to ride the horse by then but I and many others had grown up with the Hospital horse, it was good fun. Then Sister Knight came and waved us off on our way to Gran's house.

My Gran's husband, Joseph Davies, was the first person to have a taxi service in Congleton. That was in the 1930s, but he died in 1942 six years before I was born. I remember Gran complaining that day, the day she came to fetch me out of hospital, and her wishing that my Granddad was still alive just so that he could take us home in his taxi. I did too because we had somewhere in the region of over a mile and a half walk ahead of us and no transport.

We took our time on that journey though; and it was interesting. Gran made it interesting. She told me that day to always try and make good memories and lots of them, and hang onto them all. I think that is why I can always remember all of this as we went to Gran's house that day when I came out of hospital.

First there was Mrs Hibbert, she was one of my Gran's many friends, Mrs Hibbert gave me a glass of milk and some cake in the farmhouse. Mrs Hibbert and her husband owned the farmhouse and all the fields across from the hospital. Then there was the field further down Canal Road on the same side as the War Memorial. A big horse was in the field. Gran made a strange sound and the horse whinnied and came over to the fence and let us stroke it. A bit further down was a turn off called New Street. It didn't look very new to me, the houses all looked old and then there was the senior girl's school. My big sister Pauleen was going to go to that school soon. "Unless she passes her eleven-plus." My mum used to keep saying. Across from the school was what Gran called the town schools kitchens and this was where the food for the schools in Congleton was made. There was a really nice smell from there as we went past, and after that there was Townsend Road. "Is this where the town ends then?" I asked Gran. She smiled and said "No."

We came off Townsend Road and onto Park Lane where I thought all the posh people lived. "They are not posh; they only think they are." Said Gran. "Half of them haven't got two ha'pennies to rub together, hocked up to the eyeballs they are. We are the rich people, rich in worldly-wise and the nature of things."

We went up Bromley Road next and we went up the steps to Gibralter Rocks. This was where my aunty Irene lived and Gran wanted to talk to her about something. I had to stay outside. Aunty Irene's house was going to be knocked down and she was going to move to a new house on a big Council Estate in Buglawton.

After we left aunty Irene's, we met Joe Wood at the bottom of Festival Hill and Gran got talking to him. Joe Wood used to be a boxer but he was now what people call punch-drunk. He was always wandering around town. Gran always felt sorry for him and she told me that she knew him before he took up boxing. He came up to us and started talking to Gran. He was like Walter Gabriel on the wireless on the Archers programme, and he said in a croaky voice "Lydia! How are you me old pal me old beauty?" My Gran's name was Florence Lydia. We always called her Granny Lil but I never knew why. After a bit, Joe Wood seemed to lose interest in talking and went off down the road and he didn't even say goodbye to Gran and me.

We carried on up Bromley Road; this was where a lot of the factories were that I was beginning to find out about. There was Jacksons the fairground ride makers and Stott and Smiths, they made towels and nappies. There was Conlowe's and they made? Women's things. Then there was Redfern and Rheads and a few other factories but I didn't know what they made.

Gran and I were both tired out by the time we got to her house, so we had some bread and cheese and a drink and then we had a lie down together on the settee, she told me to scratch her back for her and then we both must have gone to sleep, because the next thing I remember was Gran getting up and saying she should be getting tea ready for me and her and Maurice.

Maurice was Gran's lodger and he drove buses for Bostock's Coaches. He was a nice enough man and he always told us to call him Maurice, but we knew that he could be a bit moody. He never got angry or shouted at anybody though, he just used to go quiet and wanted to be left alone. Gran told us that this was because of the War. He wasn't in when we got to Gran's house

Gran was great! I loved my Gran and everything at Gran's house. And her garden was great as well. Gran was fifty-nine in that year of 1955 so she couldn't do as much gardening as she used to do, but Maurice did what he could and Gran said that it was therapeutic for him. Gran knew where everything was in her garden and especially her herbs, but there was lots of other food-stuff as well. There were potatoes, carrots, peas and beans and onions and rhubarb, strawberries and raspberries and some apple trees right at the bottom of her garden.

Before I went into hospital, I was playing in Gran's garden one day with my brother and we played hide and seek in her raspberry canes but there were no raspberries to eat so we pulled a stick of rhubarb and tried eating that, but it made our teeth go squeaky. We knew the leaves were very poisonous.

What Gran had in her kitchen was a big oblong white sink called a Belfast sink, it stood on two piles of bricks under the window and had just a cold-water tap and there was a small table and two chairs and a green and cream painted larder unit, and a gas cooker, which was fuelled with our own gas made here in Congleton. The kitchen ceiling was a creamy white colour and the walls were painted with what Gran called 'Utility green.' This was a war-time paint that had stood the test of time. This was, after all, about ten years after the end of the second World War. Gran's house and her garden was all a world of wonder. The only place we were told never to go was in Maurice's bedroom next to Gran's bedroom.

Now that I have got this far in my story, I will try and describe the merits of how my Gran made a good wholesome, really good meal. "Just what the doctor ordered." she said to me that day, so, here we go.

First of all, we had to find what Gran called her Sussex Trug. I found it. It was under the sink behind the little curtain. It was like a cane basket but it was made out of thin strips of wood and it had a handle in the middle and that was made out of thin strips of wood as well. Gran had had this trug for a very long time and she was telling me to look after it as we stood on the garden path looking out onto her back garden.

I was seven years old, at the time. I had just come out of hospital, but there was to be no delicate treatment for me that day, or any day... Not from my wonderful Granny Lil. No! I was about to do some gardening, I was going to get my hands dirty, and I was about to have a mathematics lesson as well. Gran said for me to go and pull up just one of the potato plants and gather all the new potatoes that I could find beneath it, and then I was to go and pick twenty pea pods and ten bean pods and then to pull up one onion and then I was to pull up a small cabbage and put them all in the trug. Then I went and carried my load over to my Gran in the herb garden. This was where she pointed out the Rosemary and the Sage and something she said we are all short of, and that was; 'Thyme.' For years after, I always thought that the herb thyme was spelt 't,i,m,e'.

We put some of these herbs in the trug and then we both carried it back to her kitchen, but then she sent me outside again, to pick a bunch of mint that she had forgotten to get... to go with the... Lamb chops! Two lamb chops, and I was going to have a bit of Grans and a bit of Maurice's lamb chops. Gran told me that the mint was growing in an old galvanised bucket at the back of the herb garden. I went back outside while Gran was singing that song "There's a hole in my bucket dear Lisa, dear Lisa, there's a hole in my bucket dear Lisa a hole…"

Having got all the ingredients I somehow got the impression that I was in for a real treat as I watched Gran preparing the meal.

First of all, she chopped up the herbs and the onion, along with a sprinkle of salt and a dash of pepper and covered the lamb chops with it and put some water in as well and put a lid on the dish and then she put it in the oven.

Next came an example of cooking that has stayed with me all of these years, and I still follow Gran's system to this day.

Potatoes, (small new one's) Wash them, and put them in a pan of water with a pinch of salt and boil them for six minutes, then take them out and put them in a dish with a knob of butter and a sprig of mint. Cover and keep warm, put the chopped cabbage into the same pan and boil for two minutes, take it out and put it in another dish and keep it warm. Then cut up the beans and put them into the same pan and turn the heat off and then wait two more minutes, while you de-pod the peas.

"Freshly picked garden peas always taste better and they do you the most good, when eaten raw." Is what my Gran used to say, and I have said the same to my children and my Grandchildren too.

As I watched my Gran in her kitchen that day, it amazed me as everything seemed to happen so smoothly. I de-podded the peas for her while she took the lamb chops out of the oven. She put the chops on a plate, turned the oven off and put the plates inside. Then she poured the water from the pan into the dish the chops were in, along with a crushed up oxo cube and swirled it all around with a spoon. Then, the gravy was ready, and all the goodness from cooking the potatoes, the cabbage and the beans was in the water and none of it was wasted. Back home my mum used to do the same thing and none of the cooking water was ever wasted. My sister's used to drink the water that cabbage had been cooked in, "To put iron into their blood." is what my mum used to say.

Anyway! That day was a good day for me when I came out of hospital. Me and Gran and Maurice sat down to a really good meal that night and just to top it all I had a slice of currant bread with real butter... Delicious!

A Christmas Carol

It's not easy remembering what St Stephen's Sunday School looked like after more than half a century. It's long gone now, but I do remember that it was in Spragg Street where Bostock's bus cleaning machine now is. What I do seem to remember of our Sunday school was a single storey red brick building with an apex over the front entrance and long thin windows on both sides of the door. The inside was just one big room with wood floors and shiny dark planking halfway up the walls. The rest of the walls and the ceiling were a pale yellow.

There was a room upstairs in the attic and also a room at the back of the hall where we children were not allowed to go. We spent the best part of most Sunday afternoons in this building. There were some ladies there and they read stories from the Bible to the girls in one corner, while Mr Poole and us boys went to the other corner to have stories from the Bible read to us as well. For the first few of those early years we children all sat on the floor and then someone gave the church a lot of chairs for us to sit on, but we had to carry our chair from the back of the hall where they were all stacked up and we got shouted at if any of us dragged our chair over the floor. Sometimes the Vicar would be there and he would read to all of us. The stories from the Bible would always be themed around the time of year, Epiphany, Easter, Advent, Christmas and so on.

Sometimes the choirmaster would come and we would have a singing session and one of the ladies would play the piano, (which we were never allowed to go near, never mind touch.) I think the choirmaster had these sessions to find out which of us had good enough singing voices and to encourage those of us who did have singing voices.

'Onward Christian Soldiers' and 'There is a Green Hill Far Away.' Were the best that I liked, but my favourite hymn off all was 'All Things Bright And Beautiful.' Two of my sisters, Annette and Janet were good singers. I don't think that I was a good very good singer. Besides, I never wanted to go in the choir. I always liked it best when all those around me were singing good and loud, then I could join in and play around with the ups and downs, but not sing so loud as the others.

Every year, around November, the vicar and the choirmaster would have all of us boys and girls together and we would practice singing Christmas Carols. I remember that first session in the late Autumn of 1955 very well, very well indeed. I was an 'innocent' 7 years old and I got carried away with enthusiasm. So much so that as we walked on our way home from Sunday school, I couldn't stop singing the Christmas Carol 'Noel' Even when we met up with my stepdad after he had come out of the Albion pub I carried on singing... I got a sharp clip round my ear that day from my stepdad though... And all because I was singing that Christmas Carol a bit different... I was singing "No Hell, no Hell, no Hell no Hell."

The Carol Concert.

The year was 1961. A 13year old boy was about to climb aboard a Bostock's Coach for a Carol concert outing, organised by St Stephens Church. It seemed as if half the children of Congleton were there as well and most of them were girls... Puberty!!! That most confusing period in a young person's life. Sandra Fewtrell was there! Me and my younger brother stuck together like gluc while we went on that journey.

We were outside the church at last and about to be welcomed inside. Under the bright lights above the carved stone archway at the entrance there was a tall elderly man, with grey hair and dark interesting eyes and he smiled pleasantly at us as we went past him.

Inside that brightly lit entrance there were a lot more people and more people were coming in behind us… Sandra was up front with some other girls.

The inside of the church had white walls and dark wood, lots of dark wood, carved and decorated in such a wonderful way that I wanted to get as close as I could… and, and distract me from looking at Sandra… but I couldn't get close to the carved woodwork, I wasn't being allowed to because someone was there. A tall lady in a long red dress and with long fair hair down to her waist was showing us all into one of the many beautifully carved pews and once inside, the door on my right was closed on us. I ran my hands over the smooth ancient carved wood of the door. Then, despite all the noise going on around us I slowly became aware of a peaceful atmosphere. It shouldn't have felt strange but it did, I had been in many churches but this was a proper church, warm, cosy and inviting. The walls and the high timber roof above were very interesting. I looked all around and then at Sandra sitting next to my brother Stuart. She was so close I could almost have been able to touch her and she had her glasses off and was staring to the front as she cleaned her glasses with her skirt. I leaned forward a bit more and looked at my sister Annette. She was sitting at the far end of the pew with June, another of my sisters. Then Sandra saw me and smiled at me and then the noisy voices stopped and the music began. That first Carol was not for joining in, but some did as an organist began playing 'Oh Come All Ye Faithfull.' The lady in the long red dress came up the aisle and stopped at our pew. I leaned towards her as she said: - "Do you think you can manage with the order of service sheets you were given when you came in?"

I looked along the row at my colleagues and then back at the woman and said: - "Yes thank you." I hadn't the foggiest idea what the lady meant but I thought my answer was a grown up's sort of an answer.

They played all the old favourites that evening. 'Away In A Manger,' Once in Royal David's City,' and the whole of 'Oh Come All Ye Faithful.' There was also the traditional stories and even a candlelight procession around the inside of the church by the choir and the other vicar. Then I looked at her… 'Sandra.' It was somewhere around the start of 'Hark the Herald Angels Sing.' She looked so, so beautiful and,

and… as she sang… in a place where she belonged, somewhere loud
and Holy and yet; very serene and tranquil… She stood there singing
her beautiful little heart out, she was every inch a beautiful girl, right
down to her wonderful voice… But then! She looked at me… and for
one brief moment my voice was louder than any of those around me as I
looked to the front and sang: -   "GOD! AND SINNERS,
RECONCILED."

The Greenhouse

My stepfather once worked for a man named Horace Pointon who had a
second-hand timber yard at the bottom of Congleton Edge Road. He
used to drive a big green Foden flat back lorry for Mr Pointon and go all
around the country dismantling old 'Nissen huts.' These were wooden
buildings that had once housed military personnel during the War, and
were no longer needed. These Nissen huts, had what was called Critall
windows, they were long steel framed about four-foot six high by
eighteen inches wide, with three window panes and one at the top that
opened outwards. They are quite valuable and collectable these days.
Anyway! Me and Mum thought about it and then we decided that we
ought to build a greenhouse in the back garden, so that we could grow
more of our own produce, But! We would have to ask my stepdad…
Strangely enough, he was all for it and he even said that he would help
me to build it… "I'll have a word with Horace." he said "About a dozen
or so Crittall windows and a load of three by two timber should do it…
I'll help you build it but you'll have to pay for it lad."

I paid him but he never did help me build that greenhouse. All the
materials lay in an untidy heap for months and I very nearly severed my
Achilles tendon when frustration forced me one day to put a foot
through a pane of glass. Shortly after this little fiasco I ended up
building the damned thing myself, aye and I even taught myself to cut
glass as well. But it was all worthwhile, because that greenhouse helped
enormously with our production of good wholesome food.

By this time, in the year of 1964, our original family of eight were about to go down to six, but these were still six hungry mouths to feed. It wasn't my responsibility to feed the family but I couldn't leave it all up to my Mum, could I? Not when I was getting to be a keen gardener and poultry keeper myself at that time.

My eldest sister, Pauleen; had by now left home and she was married. I was in the greenhouse early one evening, after work, pricking out some seedlings, when Mum came and told me that June, my other elder sister, had just packed her bags and gone. This was sad but it didn't surprise me and I just carried on with what I was doing. Mum's attitude wasn't much different, when walking away from me that day I heard her saying "Ah well! one more mouth less to feed I suppose."

Congleton had a fledgling Horticultural Society around this time and one of its members was a fine man that I knew, by the name of Percy Kirk. Percy used to encourage me to go with him to their meetings at a place in Park Street. I was doing alright back home with rows of broad beans, carrots, beetroot, onions, peas and cabbages and lots more besides and I was proud of my efforts. There were even tomato plants and cucumbers and a small grape vine growing in the greenhouse. Now tomatoes! Home grown tomatoes, in those days, was a real luxury food and no mistake. The only trouble was, Percy tried to get me to enter the Horticultural Show that year. I was keen alright but there was no way that I could grow a prize-winning carrot, broad bean, tomato, or anything else! because it all got eaten as fast as I could grow it.

Highcroft Hotel

Highcroft Hotel was on the corner of Highcroft Avenue and Park Lane. It's a private house now, a very big private house. The early 1950's were times that most people did not wish to dwell upon, what with the rationing and the aftermath of the war and such. As a consequence of those hard times there was a lot of youngsters on our estate that were half starved, aye and some adults as well.

I used to spend a lot of my time on my own, just walking around. I was only seven at the time, when one day I came across half a dozen or so lads and a few girls from two of the families on the estate. They were all going one way, towards the posh houses on Park Lane. Curiosity got the better of me and I followed behind them as they went up Highcroft Avenue and then they went into the grounds of the Hotel and I watched from the gate as a man came out and started to give them some food. He saw me and called out but I ran away.

Later that day, when Mum came home from work; I told her what had happened and tried to tell her about the nice man at the Hotel but she got angry with me and said something like: -

"I spend all hours God sends, earning money, to feed and clothe you lot and you. You! go begging for food! Get upstairs right this minute… Go on!"

"But Mum!"

"Go!"

The House on the corner of Edinburgh Road and Highcroft Avenue.

The year was 1960 and I was just turned 12 years old, when one day, just at the start of spring half term holiday, my stepfather told me that he had got me a gardening job. Huh! some half term holiday that turned out to be!

Monday morning, bright and early, I was turfed out of bed and told to get ready to go with him. So go I did. It was only a short journey that morning for me and my stepdad through the gully up to the top of Dale Crescent and onto Edinburgh Road to where the newly built house was, on the corner of Highcroft Avenue and Edinburgh Road. I watched him go on his way up Highcroft Avenue and then looked at the daunting task of digging over that corner plot. It took me more than three days of hard, backbreaking toil to clear that plot of land of broken bricks, rubble and weeds and such and then to have to rake it all over so that the new owners could have a lawn sown. This was going to be a waste of good growing ground I thought and I even told the lady of the house, but I was told to get on with it and not to be cheeky.

No monetary payment, nor any other payment came my way for all that hard work though, because guess what? The man of the house was a friend of my stepdad and they both went to the same pub... The Albion.

Summer Holidays

The summer of 1957 was the first camping holiday for us as a family. In fact, it was the first ever holiday for any of us six children. We were going all the way to another country, called Wales! (so my big sister kept telling us.) well, a place in Wales, called Prestatyn, to be more precise, and we were going to get there in a very old van that Mum called "Little Betsy" It wasn't ours, it was one that Mum had borrowed from a neighbour. You could do that sort of thing in those days. My stepdad called it a rust bucket. Mum borrowed a tent as well; it was an old army tent and plenty big enough for all eight of us. We six children sat on that big white canvas tent in the back of the van and we watched the road through the holes in the floor and through the tiny windows at the back of the van. Mum and Dad were up front and Mum kept complaining that she couldn't find where we were on the map. It took a long time to get to where we were going but we got there and then we all helped to put the tent up in a big field where there were even more people and more tents. The first thing we had to do was to put the wooden poles together into something that looked like a goal post at a football match and then this went inside the canvas that was lying on the ground. Then me and my younger brother went inside to hold up the poles while Mum and Dad pulled the tent up and tied what they called the guy-ropes, down. When it was all up, the girls started to carry all our things inside while Mum sat down on the grass and started to roll herself a cigarette and I remember saying to her

"Mum, you don't have to smoke now, we are on holiday!"

She used to say that having a fag calmed her down. Dad was the same but different. Most mornings back home we would hear him getting up for work and then he would start a horrible coughing and he would say "I'll be alreet when I've had me first fag."

We were all hungry after the long drive to get to Prestatyn and that evening, we watched as Mum and Dad went off to get us all some fish and chips. There were other boys and girls at that campsite but Dad said that we were not to go outside the tent and we were to wait there until they came back with some food.

About half an hour or so later they were back, and they were arguing. I was standing by the tent flap holding it open when I heard Mum saying, "I don't know why you can't go just one time, just the one time without your ale." and then he came angrily past me and into the tent and knocked me to one side. I won't elaborate further, but suffice to say, by the time hunger took over from hurt, he was there, ordering me to eat what was by then some fish and chips wrapped up in newspaper soggy with vinegar. Even now as I write this story, more than sixty years later, I don't like the taste of vinegar on fish and chips.

The Yule-time Log.

Mr Lancaster from Daffodil Del was a really nice man. I used to spend a lot of my time in his timber yard, and the surrounding countryside, from about the age of eight, until I was turned twelve or so. I used to cycle about five miles each way. I can't remember how I came to find Mr Lancaster's place but I do know that I was very young when I did.

I never liked being in the house when Mum and my step-dad were arguing, this was one of the reasons why I used to go out so much, on my own mostly. And so, this particular day, at eight years old, I got on my bike and decided to go on an explore, a really big explore, out into the countryside… and I ended up at Mr Lancaster's… I knew straight away that he was a good man… you got to know who were the bad people and who were the good people early on when we were young. Sometimes it took some time to find out what they were like but I knew straight away that Mr Lancaster was a good man. The best of times was during the summer holidays when I could spend longer there. People used to call him Wilf, or Wilfred, but he was always Mr Lancaster to me. I think I learned a lot from Mr Lancaster, but a few years later at around the age of eleven; I was about to learn more. One day, when I was in his work-shop I asked him what the planks were for that I knew had been leaning up in a corner for years and years and were covered in cobwebs and dust. He came up to me and then he said: - "Lad... Them are a fine few planks of good old Elm... for my coffin... Aye, and I'll be making it myself one day, but not yet awhile eh!"

Later on in that same year of 1959, I helped Mr Lancaster with what he said was an age-old custom. It was nearly Christmastime and I was off school for some reason or another, and I also wasn't supposed to be in the house, for some reason or another, so, I got out my bike and headed for Swettenham.

Mr Lancaster's workshop was in an old black and white timber building; where the original wattle and daub had long since been filled in with bricks that had been whitewashed and the whitewash was falling away in places, showing some of the red bricks. The inside of Mr Lancaster's workshop was just as amazingly ancient, with lots of hand-tools and a big wooden workbench. The floor was covered in a thick layer of sawdust and all the machinery, inside and outside, was powered by the Mill waterwheel. All around the yard were stacks of planks of timber with sticks between them to let air through. Some of those stacks of timber must have been seasoning there for ten years or more. There were a few other buildings dotted around but the best one of all, outside the work-shop that is, was the cutting shed. This had a galvanised tin roof with four timber supports at the corners and was open all around. Inside this shed was a horizontal saw and there was an iron trolley that ran on steel tracks and huge logs would be rolled onto this trolley and it would then be pulled into the shed where the saw would cut the tree trunk into planks. And it was all powered by the water wheel, pulling the trolley on the rails and the cutting. All Mr Lancaster had to do was watch it going in and then he would push and pull some levers and such and then the iron trolley would be rolled back outside. I liked helping him with this bit as well. And then Mr Lancaster would go and drop the horizontal saw blade down a notch and move a lever or two and the trolley would start to be pulled back inside towards the saw blade again. This really was a fantastic place to be and what followed this particular day; was even more fantastic, when Mr Lancaster asked me if I would like to help him with the; Yule log.

In my young years, I had heard of the Yule log and of some of the traditions that went with it. The Yule log was supposed to be lit on Christmas Eve and then kept burning until the twelfth night. It must have been a really big log to burn for that long a time. There was no way that we could do that sort of thing at home, not with the size of our fire-grate!

"Come on lad." said Mr Lancaster that day. "Come and let me make you a good memory this day that will last you a lifetime."

At the back of his cutting shed was a log, a big log! It was about four feet long by a good fifteen or more inches wide, and Mr Lancaster went and tied a big long rope around one end and I helped him pull it outside and into the yard; where he told me that this was the Yule log for the big house, Swettenham Hall, at the top of the hill. Then he said that in the olden days, men would lash ropes around the Yule log and drag it up the hill and present it to the Master at the Hall. "But we don't do it like that nowadays young man… No!... we cut it up into twelve good sized logs and then we throw it in the back of the old landrover and take it up to the hall that way… Our Christmas gift to the Lord of the Manor… or what used to be called Lord of the Manor…"

By now it was getting dark, and cold, and frosty. I knew that I should really be getting off home, but I wanted to help Mr Lancaster some more, and I'm glad that I did. Just the memory of being there in his timber yard at any of the many times that I was there, was sufficient for me, and then Mr Lancaster started his big saw and cut that log into twelve chunks, or 'rings' as he called them. And a short while later, a man in a Landrover came in to the yard and we loaded the logs in at the back and my bike went on the top. Then I was given a lift, up to Swettenham Hall.

When we got there, it was proper cold and dark and there was some snow flying about. The lights at the big house were on and a woman came to the door with some drinks in glasses for Mr Lancaster and the other man, and then the Lady went back inside and came out again and gave me an orange... a real orange! We didn't very often have oranges in our house... Mum couldn't afford them... I should have saved that orange and given it to my Mum, or shared it with my brother and sisters, but I didn't, I ate it, there and then. It was snowing a lot more now, but there was a lot of happiness for the eleven-year-old me and for these other people; outside the big house that night. Some other men came and unloaded the logs and then they joined in with the happiness and I watched them all drinking and talking and there was the nice lady standing in the doorway with the light behind her. The whole thing was magical and looking at Mr Lancaster standing nearby, I remember thinking to myself, that Mr Lancaster really was creating a good memory for me that night and it is one that has lasted these many years. I didn't want to lose that moment, that wonderful moment in time but, it had to end... I knew it had to end, and then... then I was taken home... and played heck with by my Mum... and narrowly avoided a smack from my step-dad... for not telling anyone where I had gone... and for being late home and they didn't want to hear anything at all about my story, my Christmas story with Mr Lancaster... Did you?

The Co-Op

According to my Mum and my Gran, the Co-operative Society is a really amazing organisation. We were at my Gran's house one nice day early on in 1958, when Mum and Gran got talking about the Co-op and where all their shops were in Congleton. I was about nine or ten at the time and we were off school. I remember Gran giving me a piece of paper and a pencil and I was to write down the names of the streets that she was about to tell me, so that me and my brother Stuart could go and find out where all the Co-op places were.

Off we went that day... The first one was easy; it was on Bromley Road not far from Gran's house in Vaudrey Crescent and from ours in Dale

Crescent. This was the one that Mum used as well. Very often Mum would send one of us down to this Co-op for a loaf of bread and she would say something like "And don't eat the crust on your way home." But we would, it was far too tempting not to and the bread was all made here in Congleton by the Co-op. The Bakery was on that list, as well as the Slaughterhouse, and the Shoe shop, the Drapery, the Clothes shop, the Butchers, Chemists, Furniture shop... and... the Funeral parlour. Oh! and then there was the Mobile Butchers. Mum said that she knew a woman who worked in the Co-op offices in Mill Street and the books the mobile butcher used on his rounds were always covered in animal blood and this lady had to enter the customers details in a big book called a ledger once a week. Mum said that it turns this woman's stomach every time and makes her feel proper poorly. Having ticked off the Bromley Road shop, me and Stuart carried on down the bank towards Festival Hill. Across from Festival Hill is the gully that comes out at the top of Spragg Street next to Saint Stephen's school. A bit further down Spragg Street is our favourite chip shop. We only come here at special times though, mostly only when Dad gets in a good mood or when Mum does some extra overtime at work. A bit further down there's some houses and a sweet shop, we've never been in the sweet shop, this is across from our Sunday school. We were looking for Park Street and Gran said to look out for the Co-op grocers shop on the corner of Park Street in a red brick building that was made out of Accrington bricks. We found it, and a man came out and asked what were we doing. We were touching the bricks, because Gran had told us to feel how smooth they were.

We were supposed to go up Moor Lane next, to the slaughterhouse, but Stuart wanted to go down the bank to Hankinson's field to play football with some lads that were going that way. Stuart's only five; nearly six, but he's a better footballer than me. Anyway, we went down the bank with the noisy Victoria Mill on our right and the smelly chimney that my Gran said was the highest one in Congleton and was belching out big black clouds of smoke. There's a woodworker's shed a bit further down the bank where a man makes violins and such, he's got a noisy saw that cuts up pieces of timber that me and Stuart take down to him on our trolley, so as Dad can use them for nest boxes in his pigeon cote. Those lads didn't want me or Stuart to play football with them though, so we went back up the bank and a bit further up what's called Moor

Lane to where the big blue doors of the Co-op slaughterhouse are. We couldn't go in so I teased Stuart a bit by telling him that I could hear a cow in there and then we went up to have a look at the Co-op chemist on the corner of Gibraltar rocks and Park Lane. Gibraltar rocks is where my Aunty Irene used to live, before they pulled her house down. Then we went across the road past the Albion pub where Mum didn't like dad going and then we went into Lawton Street and down past Dean's Post Office and then past Oxburrows across from the Cenotaph. Oxburrows is where we get our hen food and bran from. Next to the Cenotaph is the Premier Cinema and people call it the flea-pit. There's a gent's toilet next to the flea-pit but I've never been in there because my Uncle Jim said that strange men meet up there and that I should not go near it.

Gran told us that the Co-op funeral parlour is on the corner of Canal Street across from the Town Hall. We went around to the back and saw some men taking a big brown coffin inside... one of the men told us to 'bugger off.' We weren't supposed to use that word.

We went up Chapel Street next but we didn't go in Saint Peter's church-yard, or even up the Cockshoots. We went down to the Vale instead.

There's a black and white house on the corner of the Vale and some say that it's haunted. They say that a woman lives there all on her own and the roof leaks, but I haven't ever seen her. Me and Stuart went down into the Vale and climbed the wall so that we could watch the Howty Brook waterfall as it drops down into a hole in the ground and then we got back down and went and came out on Wagg Street. This is where the next Co-op is. It's another grocer's shop. We went to the other end of Crescent Road next and came out at Astbury Street. I hadn't been around here very much but Gran said that there was a Co-op butchers down at the bottom of this road and that it was another Accrington brick building and on the corner around the front was another Co-op grocer's shop. We went down past Saint James' school and at the bottom of the street is Saint James' Church on the other corner. We soon saw the Accrington brick building and the entrance to the butcher's shop, but before that there were some men pulling boxes up on a rope that was hanging down from a beam that stuck out from the wall high up above the butcher's shop. These men told me and Stuart to keep away so we didn't go and touch the smooth bricks like we did the other one. There's a big house across the road behind a high wall and this must be the place where the new road is going to come. Uncle Jim and some other men were working on the road that was going to be called Clayton bypass. Gran said that we must come back towards the town when we had got out this far and that we should look out for Antrobus Street and at the bottom of Antrobus Street on our right, would be the Co-op bakery and all the other Co-op buildings and the offices where the boss of the Co-op works. We knew it was the bakery when we could smell the bread and such. In Mill Street is where most of the bigger Co-op shops are, we didn't go in any of them but we did have a good look and then we ticked these off our list and then we went back to Gran's house to show her what we had done.

Back at Gran's house we watched eagerly as Gran looked at the paper and then she told us that we had missed a few places but only because she had forgotten about one and didn't want us to go so far out to the others. One of the 'others' was at the top of Park Lane next to the Station, this was the CWS (Co-Operative Wholesale Society) Creamery and the other was another grocer's shop on the other side of the railway lines in a place called Hightown. The remaining one that Gran had forgotten to tell us about was at the other end of Tommy's Lane. So, away me and Stuart went once more.

Tommy's Lane is a nice place, we played down there a lot and this was the way we went to school. There was a wooden bridge across Tommy's brook and we knew we could drink the water if we wanted to. A bit further on is where Dorothy Wright lived with her Mum and Dad, it's on the way up to William Street. Dorothy was in the same class as me and she was deaf and had a black box on a belt around her waist that helps her to hear. I liked Dorothy. But me and Stuart weren't going past Dorothy's house, we were going to go the other way towards Brook Street and Church Bank.

Right across from where Tommy's Lane comes out is where the last Co-op was that Gran told us about. This was another grocer's shop and it had boxes outside with fruit and veg on display. This last Co-op for us to find, was next door to the Throstle's Nest pub and a bit lower down the bank than the Post Office on the corner of King Street. Joe Wood lives in King Street and he used to be a boxer but he was what people said 'punch drunk.' Some people used to make fun of Joe Wood but Mum always told us not to. We didn't see Joe Wood that day so, having found the last Co-op we went back to Gran's house again and then we went home.

The 'Divi'

The 'divi,' or dividend, was another fantastic part of the Co-op. If you were a member of the Co-op you were given a number, which meant that you were a part owner of the Co-operative Society and every time that you shopped in any of the stores you would give your number and that would go in a ledger and then when 'Divi-day' came around, you would be given back a fair share of the profits that the local Co-op shops had made. Or you could leave it in and let the money build up.

My Gran never spent hers and when she died in 1980 there was well over one thousand pounds in her divi-book.

Now here is a post-script to the Co-op story: -

The Selective employment tax was introduced in 1966, by a Labour Government, under Harold Wilson. It came to be known as… The none productive worker's tax. Which meant that the businesses that made things in factories didn't have to pay the tax, but those who didn't make anything, like shopworkers, did have to pay the tax. The, none productive worker's tax was designed to help Industry and boost our exports of manufactured goods, but it didn't really do any good in that respect. However, what it did do was to bring about the almost complete downfall and destruction of the entire Co-operative Society movement within this Country and closed a lot of other shops as well. The Co-operative Society. Or as my Gran would say, "The Co-op" Is… or was… a really amazing organisation." And she saw its downfall in the sixties just as we all did. The same Labour government under Harold Wilson also introduced, around the same time, the Graduated Pension scheme, which was something else that turned out to be disastrous but it would take many years for the working classes to find that out to their cost. But enough of the political diatribe. Season's Greetings and a Happy Christmas to one and all.